Being World Class

The Secret to Having a Meaningful Life

by

Dr. Joseph Schames

The cover of this book was made to elevate the neshamah of the artist's maternal grandmother, Perla Violeta Melgar.

Contents

<u>Acknowledgments</u>

I would like to give thanks to Hashem who has instilled in me this quest in compiling these thoughts and ideas to teach my children and future generations the purpose of life and how to internalize proper religious beliefs into their daily living, giving them passion and purpose for a meaningful life.

I am always filled with gratitude to all of my teachers in life, and especially to my father Rabbi Leib Schames, Z"TL, to my mother, Esther Schames, and also to my Rebbe, Rabbi Simcha Wasserman, Z"TL, where my parents and my Rebbe instilled within me meaning, purpose, and passion in life not only by their words but also by their example.

I also wish to thank my incredible Ayshes Chayil, June, our wonderful children and grandchildren, and to the people with whom I have learned Torah every week for over a decade. All of you have made me strive to be a better person.

I wish to express gratitude to Gary Kadi, the best life management consultant I have encountered, who has graciously granted me permission to use some of his ideas in this project.

I wish to express gratitude to David Lieberman, Ph.D., who through his publications and clear thinking opened my eyes to a deeper understanding of human behavior.

I wish to especially thank Cindy Kaplan, Justin Levi, Leslie Fuhrer Friedman, and Calah Hardin for all of their wisdom and input in editing this manuscript.

The personal encouragement in this project that I have received from Rabbi Moshe Mordechai Chodosh, Z"TL, Rabbi Meir Milo, and Rabbi Moshe Kesselman has been invaluable to me. Thank you.

The purpose of compiling this book is to clearly lay out to the reader a method in life of internalizing belief in God with religious principles as set forth by the

Torah, thereby living a meaningful life as a "world class" individual.

Joseph Schames

joeschames@gmail.com

Being World Class

Notes:

Why Be World Class?

An important Torah concept is "*Bishvili nivrah ha'olam*," or "The world was created for me."

This Torah concept means we have to think and feel deserving of all that life has to offer.

Rashi explains in Parshas Lech Lecha (Bereishis 12:1), when Hashem told Avram to go forth "for you," it implies that man should understand that an individual deserves the benefits and pleasures that this world has to offer; the entire world is for you.

Every individual must understand that he or she deserves all that the world has to offer. In order to get what you deserve, you have to realize that you deserve it. Everyone can achieve his or her dreams; they simply have to believe they deserve success and then take proper action to make those dreams reality. Simply having images of things you want and to think you deserve is not enough.

Notes:

Believing you deserve those things and taking proper action to get them is how to turn your dream into a reality.

To deserve and be motivated towards a goal, you must first think about it, then talk about it, and then act. Only then can it materialize in your life. Thought, speech, and then action is the way to accomplish your goals in life (Tanya, Chapter 4).

Your feelings dictate what you think about, and what you think about dictates what you deserve. If you feel great about yourself and about your future, you'll think positive thoughts, and you'll create a great life.

Attitude comes first.

Having the proper attitude in life turns an ordeal and challenge into an adventure. Having a world class attitude will give you a world class life: a life free from worry and free from doubt. Living a positive life with a positive attitude is the

Notes:

best way to make sure your time on this Earth is fulfilling and meaningful.

How does one make life meaningful?

A human being is essentially made up of three forces which are intertwined and bound up into one package. These three forces are:

1) The **Soul**, which can be described as our conscious or spiritual force (Yetzer Tov).
2) The **Ego**, which can be described as our drive for recognition and craving to be in control (Yetzer HaRah).
3) The **Body**, which represents our animalistic drives, and which always will try to persuade us to do what is easiest, most comfortable, and most physically pleasurable.

These intertwined forces which make up a human being are involved in the moment by moment struggles and decisions made by every person every second of his or her life. Hashem

Notes:

purposely created the human being with these three forces to work properly together in order for humans to reach their goals of having a meaningful and world class life.

These forces are described in the Torah in the passage, "And you shall love Hashem, your God, with all of your heart(s) (Ego), with all of your Soul, and with all of your might (Body)" (Devarim 6:5).

As Rashi comments, the word **levavecha** is written in the plural, which signifies that it describes the many drives of our competing **yetzers**, our "Soul vs. Ego." Please note in the Torah passage that the Lev/Ego force is written before the force of our Nefesh/Soul, because the ego is a stronger force to control.

The word **meodecha** stems from the word "Meod." In the Torah, *meod* has a connotation of bodily desires which, when uncontrolled, have "evilness" associated with them. (Please see the

Notes:

Ramban's explanation of "Tov Meod" Bereishis 1:31.)

The secret to a meaningful and wonderful life is that in every decision and action that we do, we should try to always have the force of our Soul control the forces of our Ego and Body.

Let us examine each force.

Soul

The Soul can be described as the conscious or the spiritual force within every person. This is the force which knows how to correctly act in every decision and action in one's life. Deep inside each of our souls we know what is correct. We only have to allow our Soul to control our decisions and to thereby guide our actions.

The Torah is our guidebook of how to utilize proper human behavior to assist the force of our Soul in controlling the forces of our Ego and Body. These three forces are in constant competition to

Notes:

"win" in all of our decisions and actions, every second of our lives.

When people use the force of their Soul to make a decision and act properly in their lives, they then automatically feel good about themselves and have self-respect. When a person continuously decides and acts, allowing the force of the Soul to win, then that person has self-esteem. Only after we allow our Soul to guide our decisions and actions, controlling the competing forces of our Ego and Body, do we then have a meaningful life.

By allowing our decisions and actions to be controlled by the force of our Soul's winning over of the forces of our Ego and Body, we then have a life free from worry and anxiety, and free from doubt.

Making proper decisions and performing actions controlled by our Soul's winning over the Ego and Body is what is meant by having freedom of choice. Hashem has given us the freedom of choice to choose which force

Notes:

is in control. It is our choice which of the three forces will win.

That is what is meant by the saying "There is no free person except if he is occupied in his performance through Torah." If one is following our Torah guidebook, then our decisions and actions will be guided by the force of our Soul, doing what is correct, and thereby winning over the forces of our Ego and Body.

In the Torah, why was Pharaoh punished over his decision to not allow the Israelites to leave Egypt? Does it not state that Hashem "hardened" Pharaoh's heart? Why was Pharaoh punished if he did not have the freedom of choice over his own actions?

The word *hichbaditi* is incorrectly translated as "hardened." Hichbaditi actually means that Hashem allowed Pharaoh the freedom of choice to make his own decisions per the force of his Ego. Hashem did so by allowing Pharaoh's *kavod* (honor) to control his

Notes:

decision. Pharaoh's decision was guided by the force of his ego of self-grandeur and honor of what other people would say of him if he allowed an unseen God to dictate to him what to do with the Israelites.

Each of us has the responsibility to use our freedom of choice to allow our force of the Soul to dictate and win over the forces of our Ego and Body in all of our decisions and actions. That is what is meant by willpower. Allowing our Soul to dictate what our actions will be, gives us self-respect and control over our lives, which in turn allows us each to have self-esteem, and then be free of anxiety, worry, and depression. This leads to a meaningful life – a life of being world class.

Secret: If you encounter a person who is angry with you or with others, do not be upset with them. Rather, have understanding and sensitivity toward them. Anger is the sign that the angry person is out of control of his or her situation or life due to having made

Notes:

incorrect decisions and allowing the forces of Ego and Body to win over the force of the Soul. The Talmud explains that if someone is easily angered, their life isn't a life, and they are never happy (*Pesachim* 113b). Be a shining example to these people by demonstrating to them what a meaningful life is, by having control, and by not responding. My Rebbe, Rabbi Simcha Wasserman, Z'TL always stressed that it takes two people to fight. If you do not allow yourself to be angry and engage in the fight with the other person, there will be no fighting.

Ego

The force of our Ego is the strongest of all the three forces. Our Ego is the drive that we have to project to others that we have the correct and proper image. Our decisions and actions are then dictated by how we may appear in certain ways to the outside world. Our Ego drives us to make decisions and to act with what we "think" makes us look good. The problem is that the force of our Ego is never satisfied, eventually

Notes:

becoming consumed by the desire for power and prestige.

Our Ego causes us to make decisions and to perform actions such as purchasing items that we cannot afford or do not really need, taking expensive or unnecessary vacations, and acting with arrogance and snobbery toward others.

Our Ego also causes us to gossip or make jokes about others. We wrongfully think that when we gossip or mock others, we are projecting the image that we are proper and righteous, because we would never act the same way the other person acted. The person who gossips thinks that he or she is projecting an image of trust because they know all the juicy details that they are personally sharing with you. In reality, the gossipmonger is a person whom others would never trust, and who is looked down upon disdainfully by others. Yet, due to the consuming drive of our Ego, we continue gossiping, trying to satiate our imagined feeling of prestige and honor. The person who mocks and jokes

Notes:

about others, in reality is insecure, where their insecurity comes from not having self- respect.

The powerful force of our Ego is that it actually changes our perception of reality. Our perception changes in that we think that how we are acting is correct and proper, as if this is how our Soul force wants us to act.

<u>Body</u>

Our Body force is extremely strong and is a key obstacle in making correct decisions and performing proper actions which the force of our Soul wishes us to do. Our Body force pushes us in the wrong direction by trying to do what is easy and comfortable and what feels good instead of doing what is truly correct and proper.

Our Body force is our drive to escape from life decisions through procrastination, sleep, and distractions. Our Body force causes us to overindulge in actions which are harmful to us in the

Notes:

long run, but are easy and comfortable for us to do right now, at this moment.

Our Body force causes us to decide and to act on how it feels at this moment, instead of what is healthy and proper for us in the future. Our Body force convinces us to overeat, to oversleep, to have illicit sex, to overindulge in improper actions such as drugs and alcohol, and to act in any harmful way, just for the thrill of the here and now, and because performing the action feels good at this moment.

The Soul's Control of the Ego and Body

The following is the axiom of how a human being operates. If your decisions and actions are dictated by your Soul Force, you will be content and happy. If you make your decisions dictated by the forces of your Ego or Body, you will be anxious, depressed, and feel out of control.

<u>Notes:</u>

When a person is feeling out of control they become angry. Anger is where one tries to gain control by feeling more powerful, where in fact this is an illusion, and the person is really out of control.

Unfortunately, when we follow the advice of our Ego and Body forces, we are never satisfied, and like a junkie, we continue to spiral in a downward fashion, becoming anxious and depressed, because deep inside our sub-conscious (our Soul) we know that we are not acting correctly. That is why we see in our world how so many people who have money and fame are depressed, unhappy, addicted, alcoholic, and even commit suicide. They value power and prestige as their goals, but they have no true meaning in their lives.

A meaningful life only comes from doing what is correct and responsible according to what our Soul force wishes us to do. When you do what is right, you feel good about yourself. You then gain self-respect. The more self-respect you have, the more self-esteem you will have.

Notes:

The more self-esteem you have the more you love yourself.

It is a given in the Torah that every person must love himself or herself. The Torah states, "Veahavta lereacha komocha" ("and you should love your neighbor as you love yourself"). This means that it is a given and readily understood that you must love yourself. How does a person learn to love him or herself? Only by making decisions and acting as dictated by the Soul force do people love themselves, because they are then happy with themselves.

In Pirkei Avot (1:6), it states, "Ase lecha rav," which many people incorrectly interpret to mean "make for yourself a mentor." The Torah (Bereishis 45:28) describes that when Jacob realized that his long lost son, Joseph, was alive, Jacob announced to his family, "Rav, od Yosef chai," or "I have happiness, Joseph still lives." We, therefore, see that the word "Rav," as grammatically written in Pirkei Avot, does not mean "Make for

Notes:

yourself a mentor," but rather, it means that you must, "make yourself happy!"

Happiness only comes after succeeding at the hard effort of acting correctly and thereby respecting yourself.

All of our decisions and actions in life must be performed by the force of our Soul controlling the forces of our Ego and Body. Hashem knew what He was doing by creating us also with the 'negative' and 'evil' forces of our Ego and Body, because they are important parts of our makeup, and when controlled, these forces help us reach even higher goals. For example, if we did not have our Body force of a sexual drive, we would not have the desire and goals of getting married and having children. If we did not have our force of our Ego, we would not strive to achieve greater accomplishments of building up our world. The Ego and Body forces are intricate parts of our complicated makeup, but our challenge in all aspects and moments of our lives is to make our

Notes:

Soul force be in control of the forces of our Ego and Body drives.

Notes:

Purpose

People are placed on earth to fulfill a purpose. There is a meaning to life where each person is tasked with some sort of contribution to society. My Rebbe, Rabbi Simcha Wasserman Z"TL, always taught that every person in the world must be a producer and not a taker.

There is nothing more important than recognizing that each and every individual on Earth was created to fulfill some sort of task in the greater world – to contribute something to society. The motivation to achieve one's purpose propels the individual to learn, grow, and most importantly, do. A life without purpose is a life of complacency, and complacency can only yield stagnation. Success is often defined as attaining one's purpose – achieving something, becoming something, creating something.

Being world class is, in its essence, tapping into your individual purpose and

<u>Notes:</u>

radiating that purpose to all those you encounter.

What, then, is an individual's purpose in life? The prophet Micah has told us what the purpose of life is:

> "He has told you, O man, what is good, and what the Lord seeks from you: only the performance of justice, the love of kindness, and walking humbly with your God."

The great sage, Rabbi Hillel, when asked to summarize the purpose of life in one simple concept (while standing on one foot), explained:

> "What is distasteful to you, do not do to another. The rest of the Torah is instructional. Now go forth and study."

Rav Chaim Volozhiner, the student of the Vilna Gaon, would frequently emphasize to his son the fundamental axiom of life as:

Notes:

"The ultimate purpose of man in this world is to better other people's lives in every way possible."

The Torah describes Enoch, who lived between the time of Adam and Noah:

"And Enoch walked with God and was no more" (Bereshis 5:24).

The Midrash describes the mighty deeds that Enoch did to receive such an accolade in the Torah:

"Enoch was a shoemaker and with each and every stitch, he forged mystical unions with his Creator" (Midrash Talpiot).

Rabbi Yisrael Salanter explains this Midrash as follows:

"The intent of the Midrash is not that at the time he stitched the shoes, Enoch was delving into the thoughts of God. Rather, the "mystical unions" that he forged came about because he put his

Notes:

entire mind and heart into each and every stitch, making certain that it was good and strong so that the shoes themselves would, in fact, be good shoes. All this he did for the benefit of his customer, in order to give the customer the pleasure of having a fine pair of shoes. As such, Enoch was able to attach himself to God by making himself more like God in character, seeing as God, too, desires to do good and to give pleasure to others. Enoch forged mystical unions with God because all that he wanted was to attach himself to God by mimicking His divine attributes" (Michtav Me'Eliyahu).

The above texts all point to one simple answer: the purpose of life is

to serve others.

Notes:

Please Note: The Torah commands us in the fourth of the Ten Commandments; "Six days you shall work and you shall perform all of your work. And on the seventh day you shall observe Shabbat.."

Our Rabbis define *melacha*, or "work," as having three requirements. In order to be considered as having performed a melacha on Shabbat, a person must have satisfied the following three requirements in their action:

- Awareness
- Intent
- Purpose

The definition of work, during the week or on Shabbat, is to have awareness, intent, and purpose in every action that we perform. In order to fulfill our purpose in life of serving others, all of our actions must be done carefully with awareness, intent, and purpose.

Interestingly, the word *melacha* is a conjunction of the words "Maleh Kah," –

Notes:

"Full of the Shechinah of Hashem." When we perform our work carefully by serving others with awareness, intent, and purpose, then our work is considered to be filled with Hashem's presence.

Notes:

The Value System

One is able to serve others by having a strong value system. The Torah provides an instructional framework for such values, and through study of its text, one can understand and live its values. In fact, the Torah is often referred to as *Torat Chaim*, which is translated as "the way of life" or "the living Torah." It's a guide that outlines morals and behaviors that embody those morals. The Torah's mandates are geared toward the relationships people have with one another. These mandates outline specific ways in which one can serve others and treat others like the equals that they are.

Hashem has challenged us to be the *Ohr L'goyim*, the "Light unto the nations," or alternatively, the "Light unto other individuals."

A beacon of light in the darkness of the world attracts all others to its glow. We become the beacon of light by serving as an example to others, by living

Notes:

exemplary lives, and by becoming world class.

Notes:

Integrity

The cornerstone of becoming world class is having integrity. Integrity is more than honesty or truthfulness. Integrity can be defined as wholeness.

One gains integrity by staying faithful to agreements. A world class individual is someone who:

- Lives within his or her integrity, by keeping agreements.
- Is bound by his or her agreements with God, with him or herself, and with others.
- Only makes commitments within his or her value system and remains committed to said commitments.

That's where wholeness lies. Conflict can only occur when agreements are not maintained. Living outside your integrity

Notes:

– for instance cheating on a spouse or in a business deal – is essentially acting selfishly and taking advantage of others, instead of serving them. Truly world class people, living with their integrity, are without conflict because they keep their agreements.

This is further demonstrated by the word for wholeness in Hebrew, *Shalom*. Shalom is often translated as "peace." When we wish Shalom to the people we meet and we pray that God bless us with Shalom, we are wishing them integrity. Integrity is a cornerstone to being world class.

Integrity and Agreements

If we understand integrity as a commitment to one's agreements, let us further examine what agreements we make and what agreements we must keep?

Notes:

First, we must keep our agreements with God. The Torah repeatedly states that the main agreement that we have with God is to recognize, understand, and have complete belief that "Hashem Hu Ha'Elokim, Ein Od Milvado," which means, "Hashem is the one and only God, there is no other except Him."

The credo of "Shema Yisroel" is a declaration of this concept. Every commandment in the Torah that is between man and God has its source and purpose to remind us that Hashem is the one and only God. Even the remainder of the commandments, which deal with obligations of man to his fellow, has its source as recognizing that man is created "B'tzelem Elokim," that is, "in the image of God," and, thereby, should make a person remember his foundational agreement with God that there is no other besides Hashem.

Notes:

As long as we keep this agreement with God, we maintain our integrity with Him. This is the only major agreement that God wishes us to uphold with Him, and it is the only foundational belief stated in Tanach, as the prophet Habakuk states, "and a righteous individual in his belief shall he live."

Besides this one foundational agreement that man must keep with God, God has made separate other covenants with us called a "Brit," which He will never break with us, and which we must also uphold, such as the Brit of circumcision, and the Brit of Shabbos. These Britot are covenants which will never be broken by God or the Jewish People. They serve to remind us of our unique and beloved relationship with God and help us demonstrate our belief in Him.

Secondly, we must keep our agreements with others. Agreements

<u>Notes:</u>

with others include expressed and implied agreements that are actually made or expected between one human being and another. When a man marries his wife, or if he makes a verbal or contractual agreement with another, they each are involved in making a **kinyan**. A Kinyan can be translated as "creation," as it is said in the beginning of the daily prayer, Shemonei Esreh, that Hashem is **Koneh Hakol**, that is, the "the creator of everything." Making an agreement with another is "creating." It creates trust and a bond. Thus, not maintaining our agreements with others is destroying. When one doesn't hold up his or her end of an agreement, that trust is destroyed, and the bond severed.

We also have implied agreements between ourselves and all of our fellow teammates in life. Whether or not we have a relationship with every one we meet in the world, we still have implied and unwritten agreements with them to

Notes:

recognize the **Tzelem Elokim** – the inner divinity that we all possess, respecting that divinity within every person in the world. When you recognize the Godliness in each individual, when you appreciate that when you stand before your fellow man you are standing before an essence of God, you will be kinder, more respectful, and indeed, world class.

For instance, it is an obligation to greet everyone we meet with a salutation accompanied with a smile and a countenance on our faces that shines with beauty. Our sages explain in the Talmud in Berachos 6B, "Anyone who does not return a greeting is called a thief." As it says in Yeshayahu 3:14, "And you have consumed the vineyard; the stolen item of the poor is in your home." Even a poor person can become a victim of theft if you ignore him and do not present him with a proper greeting that he deserves. At the end of the day,

Notes:

the poor man is not any different than the rich man; both are wealthy in their Tzelem Elokim.

A world class person also keeps his or her agreements with others by arriving on time. Punctuality is a way of showing respect and honoring the other's time. Lateness severs the trust between two parties and causes a rift in one's integrity.

The third kind of agreement you must keep is with yourself. Ignoring agreements and commitments made to oneself leads to discomfort, self-deprecation, and negativity. Remember, if everyone is created B'Tzelem Elokim, you are, too, and by not committing to and caring for yourself, you are defacing the Godliness within you.

Moreso, a person who is not comfortable in his or her own skin or who is not happy cannot exude comfort or

Notes:

happiness to others, and cannot adequately serve others. Being happy is a moral commitment and agreement that we are obligated to show to others, and is also a personal mandate for us in order to fulfill our purpose in life. No one follows the example of a person who is not happy and who does not have his or her own life together. Happiness can only be present by having meaning, purpose, and joy in our mission in life. Serving others, therefore, does not involve neglecting yourself – in fact, it's just the opposite.

The fourth kind of agreement has to do with our morals and values, or, in other words, our agreement to follow the Torah.

The word Torah actually means "Passion." God has given us an instructional guide for us to follow with passion and desire. This emotional drive should be manifested in us like any other

Notes:

of our inborn drives, such as our inborn instincts. The Torah uses the words *v'loh taturu* when it discusses how we are not to stray after our inborn instinct towards forbidden sexual relationships. *Taturu* has the same root word as Torah; veering toward forbidden relationships is an act of passion, as is following the Torah. However, it's a question of how you channel that passion – toward the righteousness of the Torah by acting according to your Soul, or toward man's desires for debasement of the Ego or Body?

We all have passions, where each passion must be directed towards our purpose in life to serve others, and not to be misdirected away from this purpose. Every passion that we possess can be directed, guided, and used for a beneficial purpose in serving others.

Becoming world class is totally doable. Up until now, we've discussed

Notes:

conceptual ways one becomes world class, but there are specific steps one can take to achieve that level of respect. And the best part is that becoming world class is not limited to just a few individuals. Anyone and everyone can – and should – strive to become world class. The techniques discussed below are applicable to all.

World Class Qualities

Notes:

Yiras Hashem – Seeing and Recognizing God

"Raishis Chachmah Yiras Hashem." "The beginning of wisdom is to see and recognize God."

Yiras Hashem is explained by most people as "fear of God." This is incorrect. God does not want man to constantly tremble and to be afraid of Him. This is not within our mutual agreement, and it definitely is not realistic.

Rather, Yiras Hashem means **seeing and recognizing** God's presence. The root of the word, Yirah, means "to see." When we see and acknowledge every aspect and breath of our life, our surroundings, and the wonders of the universe, we then recognize the awesomeness of God. Yiras Hashem means that we are to be struck with "awe" of God.

Notes:

"Mah Hashem Elokecha Shoel Meimoch Ki Im Leyiroh" (Devarim 10: 12), means "what Hashem, your God, asks of you is to see him." Our great sage, Rabbi Meir, explained that we should not read this word "mah" as "what," but rather "meah" – "one hundred." In order to recognize and be awe inspired of God, we are to stop ourselves at a minimum of one hundred times each day, throughout the day, and make a **brachah** (a blessing), before every action we perform. A blessing acts as a speed bump in our daily life, to slow us down and stop, allowing us to be inspired with the awe of God and His creations.

When you live your daily life in this fashion, then you recognize your place in the universe relative to God. The word **Makom**, (the Place), is one of God's names. When we recognize our place in relationship to God, we then attain the wisdom of not becoming arrogant.

Notes:

Arrogance means that an individual thinks too much of himself and proves that he does not see and recognize God. If one does not see and recognize God, then he does not truly believe in Him. According to our Sages, arrogance is therefore equivalent to worshiping idols.

Arrogance proves that an individual is not world class. By seeing and recognizing the awesomeness of God, true wisdom can be achieved, and this is the beginning of being world class.

Notes:

Hodoah – Having Gratitude and Bestowing Compliments

The second quality of the world class individual is complete gratitude. The word **Hodoah** means "gratitude," and also means "praise."

It is easy to understand that we must have gratitude for any goodness that is bestowed upon us. However, our Sages explain that the same way that we are to have gratitude for the goodness of life, we are also required to have gratitude to God for any tragedy as well. Why God has allowed life to contain tragedy, as well as our requirement to have gratitude for the tragedies of life, are impossible concepts to understand with our finite minds, but belief in God ultimately must be manifested in our surrendering to God's will. The attitude we have when presented with tragedies and struggles is our challenge.

Notes:

Rabbi Joseph B. Soleveitchik, Z"TL, writes:

> *"Faith in God means having complete reliance without any reservations, conditions, or qualifications. In other words, one must have complete trust that God will never betray you. But this also means that from time to time, the faithful person must suspend judgment and act illogically and irrationally. At times a person must act in a certain fashion even though he or she does not understand why they are required to conduct themselves in such a manner. A person must appreciate that he or she cannot understand or comprehend everything. To be a true believer you must master this concept."*

Our challenge in life is to have the correct attitude in how we greet each

Notes:

tragedy and test what life has in store for us. Our challenge is to greet them with gratitude and not to abandon our belief in God.

A "great attitude" is summed up in the word "gratitude."

As you see, having gratitude is not so easy. That is why our prayers throughout the day are replete with a myriad of expressions of gratitude. This is done to help remind us every moment; every evening, every morning, and every afternoon, to have gratitude for all of God's goodness, miracles, and wonders.

As explained above, Hodoah also means "praise." God does not require our gratitude or any of our praises! Believing that He does actually belittles God. Rather, the bestowing of gratitude and praise throughout our prayers serves to train us to have the world class quality of bestowing gratitude and

Notes:

compliments to our fellow man; to everyone we meet in life.

It seems so easy for us to criticize. In fact, when we criticize we tend to create a long, drawn out story, filled with all the juicy descriptions and details of our criticism.

We must train ourselves in showing our gratitude by complimenting others with sincerity. Compliments should be drawn out with details and praise. Every person has an ego that needs to be stroked. No one is so oversensitive as to refuse a compliment.

A world class person compliments others with sincerity, recognizing the unique gifts and inner beauty the other person possesses, and thanking the other person for sharing those gifts. If we each trained ourselves to show sincere gratitude and compliments to the teammates in our lives, the world would

<u>Notes:</u>

be a less contentious place. A bully would never bully. A spouse would never stray. When you feed one another's egos with compliments on a daily basis, your ego will be more than satisfied and your spouse will be the most beautiful and wonderful person on God's planet. That is why the word for love in Hebrew is Ahavah. The source of this word is 'Hav,' 'to give.' Love is giving. Giving (and receiving) gratitude and compliments keeps love alive.

Showing gratitude and bestowing compliments are major qualities of being world class. Conversely, complaining about life detracts from a world class persona.

It's very easy to complain, and it's fun, too. Complaining gives us a superiority complex, because we determine we are better and we'd do better than whomever we belittle with our complaints. For instance, if you complain about poor service in a restaurant, you are

Notes:

essentially saying, "I would be a better waiter. If this were my job, I'd make sure to bring the food on time." And thus, with one simple complaint, we've belittled another person and elevated our own ego.

At least that's what it seems like on the surface. Complaining may make us feel better, but arrogance actually limits us and makes us less world class.

It is not that a world class person has to suffer the consequences of mistakes or actual complaint-worthy issues. Rather, a world class individual quietly and respectfully handles the situation without making a big deal and spreading bad vibes. For a world class person, pointing out a problem is the first step to finding a solution; it has nothing to do with bolstering his or her own self-worth. A world class person spends more energy on compliments than complaints,

Notes:

on solutions rather than problems, and
on loving rather than criticizing.

Notes:

Rachmonos – Having Compassion

A world class person has compassion. He or she not only understands what another person is feeling, but also listens and cares about what another has to say.

What does it really mean to experience compassion? The answer can actually be found in the Hindi word **Namaste**. Namaste means "the divinity in me salutes the divinity in you."

Every person has a pure soul within them, a Tzelem Elokim, which was fashioned in the image of God. This is the individual's divinity. A world class person recognizes the divinity in others and connects to it. How is this done in practice?

A world class person tries to relate to the divinity in everyone he or she meets. He looks for the humanity in everyone, for the essence that makes each person individual and real. He recognizes that there is no such thing as a little person.

Notes:

All people are worthy. All people have a divinity, a pure Neshama (soul) within. The world class person is, therefore, sensitive in every way possible as to not hurt another's feelings. Understanding that basic fact of existence is the secret to being a compassionate human being.

Anyone who engages with a world class person can sense his or her compassion and sincerity, and naturally relates back in a similar way. It's the mirror effect: people approach others the way they themselves are approached.

Or, in other words, their divinities salute each other.

Notes:

Anivus – Acting with Certainty, Confidence, and Courage

The fourth characteristic of a world class individual is **Anivus**, or humility. Usually, we picture a humble person as one who is meek, quiet, and has his head held low. That seems antithetical to someone who is world class.

The Torah says that Moses was the humblest person in the world. Yet, the first action that the Torah describes Moses doing is killing the Egyptian who was harming an Israelite. Killing sure does not seem to be the action of a humble person! The Torah then describes Moses' next two interactions of becoming involved with others: Moses steps in and takes a stand when two Jews are fighting, and then again when foreign people are fighting over water rights. Moses, the humblest person, becomes involved and takes a

Notes:

stand; always fighting for what is correct and just.

Anivus actually means that a person should act with certainty, confidence, and courage in knowing that his or her actions are correct, no matter what other people say. Humility means not caring about our egos and what others may say (good or bad) when he knows that his actions are correct. A humble person is actually an individual with action and purpose. He or she is the leader that others are attracted to, always knowing that the humble person does the right thing.

Humility is doing the right thing *simply because it is the right thing to do*, not because it will bring glory or notoriety. On the other hand, arrogance is doing something – whether it is the right thing or not – because the ego says it is the right way to garner accolades or press.

Notes:

Avraham Avinu (Abraham) said "Hineni," ("Here I am"), meaning "Here I am, ready to do the right thing, whatever God requests, with certainty, confidence, and courage." Avraham did not care that he was alone in his belief of monotheism, and that others would mock him. Humility is not caring what others may say when you are certain and confident that you are correct. (Please see Rashi explaining the word "Hineni"; Bereishis, Parshas Vayerah, Perek 22, Pasuk 2.)

A person with anivus should act with certainty, confidence, and courage in knowing that his or her actions are correct, no matter what other people say. By doing so, he sets an example for others to join the "world class club."

<u>Notes:</u>

<u>Chachmah – Being a Visionary</u>

Another element of a world class person is being a visionary.

Our Sages explain that being a wise person is being able to see what is going to be *born* in the future. And what is always going to be *born* in the future? ***Opportunity***.

A true visionary is someone who can see the past and the present clearly, and uses knowledge from that vision to anticipate and seek the opportunities that the future is bound to bring.

A visionary learns from his or her experiences and tries not to make the same mistake twice. Thus, every situation is really an opportunity for growth, success, and learning, not a stumbling block or rut. It's not that a visionary can predict the future, but rather, a visionary looks toward the future at all times, taking past and present

<u>Notes:</u>

experiences and using them as building blocks for a successful future.

A world class individual must be a visionary, taking care to notice the details of his or her experiences. He or she lives in a state of heightened awareness, which, in turn, gives life more meaning and, like we explained earlier, purpose.

Notes:

Ratzon – Willingness and Being Open to Learning

A world class person has a propensity toward willingness; he or she is solution-oriented. If given a task that seems too difficult or impossible, a world class person will make it work and, in his or her capacity as a visionary, use the task as a learning experience.

Many people have a "yes, but" mentality, always coming up with the reasons something simply cannot work. Many people focus on the problem. A world class person focuses on the solution, and has a "yes" attitude, and accepts every suggestion with grace. A world class person has an opportunistic attitude, always willing to try new experiences, and is always open to living a full life.

Notes:

Coexistence and Tolerance

The seventh characteristic of the world class individual is to be able to coexist with and tolerate others. Too often, people feel that they can only be right if someone else is wrong. That's where self-righteousness, arrogance, and snobbery live. A world class person, on the other hand, does not want to belittle anyone. As outlined above in our discussion of humility, he or she does what is right regardless of what anyone else does, without the motivation to take anyone down.

A world class individual makes space for people who have different opinions, philosophies, practices, and actions. It is of no consequence to the world class person if someone else disagrees with his or her opinion. In fact, the world class person would see any disagreement as an opportunity for discussion and growth. He sees the divinity in everyone,

Notes:

even those who oppose him. In this way, such an individual is at peace with his neighbors and surroundings.

There is a spectacular word in the Zulu language, a word which encompasses so much meaning. The word is **Ebantu**. Ebantu means "I am because we are." A world class person understands that co-existence and participation with others only enhances the human experience. Hillel expressed this same thought by saying, "If I am for myself, then what am I?" (Pirkei Avot. 1:14)

People are afraid of an **Ayin Harah**, the "Evil Eye." Contrary to what people think, an "Evil Eye" is not what someone sends your way, rather it is that with which we foolishly view others through our own eyes. When we view others through eyes of jealousy and intolerance, or if we are tale-bearers or gossipmongers, then we lead a shallow

Notes:

life and eventually become disgusted with our own existence. The ill-will you feel toward another person actually leads to your own degradation. We must, therefore, view everyone through a "Good Eye," always tolerating others' existence, without jealousy and with respect toward our neighbors who occupy our surroundings in life.

Our Rabbis explain that fish do not have an "Evil Eye." In fact, our forefather, Jacob, blessed his descendants to be as "a multitude of fish in the midst of the world." What does this mean?

If you have ever observed fish swimming and living in an aquarium or in any body of water, you may note that fish swim and seemingly glide through their surroundings not caring about any other fish that inhabit their surroundings. They tolerate every other fish's existence in the water.

Notes:

What is jealousy?

Jealousy is where you become angry that the other person has something that you wish you had. In actuality the anger is misplaced. The anger should really be directed against God. Why did God allow the other person to win the lottery instead of you? Aren't you as deserving as he is? Jealousy stems from a lack of "Bitachon," trust in God. Jealousy is not a sin, but rather, jealousy is _your_ punishment for not having true trust in God that He will provide for you all that you really need. This punishment of jealousy turns into a nonsensical hatred, and turns you into a person having an 'Evil Eye', which devours your every thought and unfortunately becomes your reason for existence. Wasting your life with such nonsense is then truly a punishment.

Notes:

Being world class means you must tolerate and co-exist with everyone, with all of your teammates in life. You must be happy with what they have and with what God has provided for you. "Who is a rich person? A rich person is one who is happy with their allotted portion" (Pirkei Avot. 4:1).

Notes:

Being World Class

Once you master the characteristics of being world class, it's important to build an environment for yourself conducive to maintaining and nurturing your status.

Halachah explains that a *Talmid Chacham* – a world class scholar – must be impeccably clean. A clean desk, a clean home, and a clean car are signs of being world class. Since the world class individual recognizes his or her own divinity, he or she creates a space that is fitting for that divinity. It need not be flashy; rather, it can be comfortable and well put together. A world class person is not disheveled, but instead takes care to be presentable so as to allow his or her light to shine through, unaffected.

Additionally, a world class person ought to surround him or herself with

<u>Notes:</u>

other world class or emerging world class individuals. It is too easy to get sucked into a life of arrogance, complaints, closed-mindedness, and intolerance when you are only engaged with people who have that mindset.

We are taught "Oy L'rasha, oy l'shecheino," or "Woe to the evildoer, woe to his neighbor." Someone who is in too close proximity to evil will often be influenced by that evil and become one with it. It is not that people who are not world class are evil, but the principle that one's neighbors affect him or her rings true. If you, as a world class individual, can't help but be surrounded by people who do not share your values, it is imperative to try to be their behavioral guide – not with preaching, as that is antithetical to world class behavior and borders on being self-righteous, but rather by living your life as an example that those around you can't help but mimic. We are similarly taught, "Tov

<u>Notes:</u>

l'tzadik, tov l'shecheino," or "Good to the righteous person, and good to his neighbor." The world class person must strive to embody the latter ideal.

Notes:

Looking at the Future from the Future – The End Game

A huge aspect of being world class, and continuing on a world class path, is the knowledge that you will leave behind a legacy. A world class individual is a visionary who is able to see the future. To maintain a world class lifestyle, one must look towards his or her own future, and into what will be left after he or she passes, or in other words, *what your end game will be*.

To do this, the world class individual must look back upon his or her life from the perspective of his or her deathbed. Imagine your future as though it has happened; given the visionary that you've become, you know where your past and present are leading you. Is that path satisfying to you on your deathbed? Is that how you want to be remembered?

Let this perspective, of looking at your future end game to guide your present actions, guide you throughout your world class life. What mistakes do you want to

Notes:

avoid? Which actions will you regret taking and which will you regret not taking?

In fact, Teshuvah – the return to righteousness – is detaching from your sins of the past and focusing on how you can turn the present into a moment of value, righteousness and closeness with God by living your present and future world class life guided by your end game.

Detach from your past wrongdoings and non-world class life, and live your present and future life guided by how you view your end game. That is Teshuvah.

Conclusion

Notes:

People who are world class, also have a strong sense of responsibility to themselves and to those around them — their family members and their world. These individuals are all about contribution. They do not put themselves first, but they reap the success of which selfish people can only dream. World class people are generous. They know that the more they serve others, the more they receive. They are not bashful or self-deprecating, but rather appreciative of life and the gifts God has bestowed upon them and everyone. They experience an extraordinary level of freedom — they love their work but they do not feel chained to their occupation or enslaved to money. They trust themselves and others. They act promptly and they keep their word. As a result, they have that sense of peace of mind and trust which everyone wishes he or she could enjoy. When you become world class, you will always have passion in life, finding everything in life to be exciting and to be an adventure.

<u>Notes:</u>

Being world class can be difficult to achieve and to maintain. To do so, follow this simple practice: before any action you take, and before any thought you speak, ask yourself whether a world class person would behave or speak this way? If the answer is no, then do not act or speak that way.

Let me conclude with the words of the Mishnah in Pirkei Avot (2:21):

"Lo alecha hamlacha ligmor v'lo ata ben chorin l'hibotel mimena," or, "It is not on you to finish the work, but you are also not free to avoid the work."

This means that we should be careful never to take an all or nothing approach. Instead, we must work with patience and diligence to do what we can, knowing we will not complete every single task, and pray that Hashem crown our efforts with success. A world class individual understands that the journey and process of service is one that requires

Notes:

patience, commitment, help from God, and tremendous perseverance.

Now go forth, be world class, and enjoy a meaningful life!

Summary

Notes:

World Class Individuals (WCI) have:

1. **Deserving and positive attitude**. WCI have a tremendously high '"self deserving level." They believe that they are worthy of "having it all."

2. **A tremendous sense of divine purpose**. WCI understand the challenge of having their Soul control their Ego and Body forces, and know that their purpose in life is to serve others.

3. **Integrity**. WCI honor their agreements with Hashem, with themselves and with others. They honor their agreements with Torah. WCI are able to channel their natural passions into furthering their purpose of life, which is to serve others.

4. **Yirat Hashem**. WCI see and recognize Hashem. Therefore, they have no arrogance.

Notes:

5. **Hoda'ah**. This has three parts. WCI surrender to the will of Hashem even when He tests them by doing something they can't understand. WCI bestow gratitude and sincere compliments upon their fellow man. WCI feel no need to complain or put others down.

6. **Rachmanut.** WCI respect the divinity in everyone.

7. **Anivus**. WCI feel no ego, no self-doubt, no care or concern about what others say, no sense of obligation to do more than they can, and no shame. Instead WCI feel certainty, courage and confidence.

8. **Chachma**. WCI see opportunity in every situation.

9. **Ratzon**. WCI are open to trying new things, learning new concepts, exploring new ideas and trying different perspectives.

Notes:

10. **Tolerance**. WCI are tolerant and don't feel self righteous. They are not distracted or threatened by the "small stuff."

11. **A clean and sustaining environment**. WCI have a world class environment because they create no disturbances, and they surround themselves with other WCI. WCI are impeccably clean. They feel no envy, jealousy or hatred.

12. **Teshuva**. WCI detach themselves from their past and live their lives by looking at their future end game.

The great sage, Rabbi Hillel, would always end his words of advice with the saying, "Now go forth and study." I encourage you, the reader, to do the same. Your journey in life, being a world class person, has only begun.

Glossary

- **Ahavah** — Hebrew word for 'love'. See page 95.

- **Anivus** — Hebrew word for 'humility'. See page 105.

- **Ase lecha rav** — A passage from Pirkei Avot 1:6 meaning 'to make yourself happy'. See page 39.

- **Avinu** — Hebrew word meaning 'our father'. Referring to our patriarch, Abraham. See page 109.

- **Avram** — The Hebrew name of the patriarch 'Abram' before God renamed him as Abraham. See page 109.

- **Ayin Harah** — Hebrew word for 'the evil eye'. See page 119.

- **Ayshes chayil** — Hebrew words for a 'woman of valor'. See page 6.

- **Berachos** — The name of the first tractate of the Talmud, Seder Zeraim. See page 69.

- **Bereishis** — Hebrew name for 'Genesis'. See page 109.

- **Bishvili nivra ha'olam** — Hebrew phrase meaning 'the world was created for me'. See page 11.

- **Bitachon** — Hebrew word for 'trust and security in God'. See page 123.

- **Brachah** — Hebrew word for 'blessing'. See page 83.

- **Brit/ Britot** — Hebrew word for 'covenant/s'. See page 65.

- **B'Tzelem Elokim/ Tzelem Elokim** — Hebrew phrase that means we all possess a divine spark within us, or that we are all made 'in God's image'. See page 69.

- **Chachmah** — Hebrew word for 'wisdom'. See page 111.

- **Devarim** — Hebrew word for 'Deuteronomy'. See page 17.

- **Halachah** — Hebrew word for 'Jewish laws'. See page 127.

- **Hashem** — The Hebrew name for 'God,' literally translated as, 'The Name'. See page 6.

- **Hashem Hu Ha'Elokim, Ein Od Milvado** — Hebrew phrase from Deuteronomy (4:35) that means, 'God is the one and only God, there is no other except Him.' See page 63.

- **Hav** — Hebrew word meaning 'to give'. See page 95.

- **Hichbaditi** — Hebrew word that is commonly translated to mean 'I have hardened,' but also means 'I have bestowed honor'. See page 23.

- **Hineini** — Hebrew word that means, 'Here I am, willing and ready.' See page 109.

- **Hodoah/ Hoda'ah** — Hebrew word that means 'gratitude' and 'praise'. See page 87.

- **Kavod** — Hebrew word for 'honor'. See page 23.

- **Kinyan** — Hebrew word that commonly means 'acquiring'. See page 67.

- **Koneh Hakol** — Hebrew phrase meaning that God is the 'creator of everything'. See page 67.

- **Lech Lecha** — Hebrew phrase from the book of Genesis (12:1) meaning 'go forth for yourself'. See page 11.

- **Lev** — Hebrew word meaning 'heart'. In the Bible, it refers to the 'Ego'. See page 17.

- **Levavecha** — Hebrew word meaning 'your heart(s)'. See page 17.

- **Mah HaShem Elokecha shoel meimoch ki im leyiroh** — A Hebrew phrase meaning, 'What does God ask of you except to fear Him". See page 83.

- **Makom** — Hebrew word meaning 'the Place'. It is used as a name for God. See page 83.

- **Maleh Kah** —Hebrew words for 'full' and 'God's divine presence'. See page 53.

- **Meah** — Hebrew word for '100'. See page 83.

- **Melacha** — Hebrew word meaning 'work'. See page 51.

- **Meodecha/ Meod** — Hebrew word for 'your body/ body' or 'might'. See page 17.

- **Michtav Me'Eliyahu** — Literal translation is 'Letters from Eliyahu'. It is a compilation of lectures, on Jewish thoughts written by Rabbi Eliyahu E. Dessler, Z'TL, titled "Strive for Truth". See page 49.

- **Midrash** — The ancient commentary on the Torah, dating to a time before the 2nd century CE. It contains metaphors that elaborate on incidents in the Torah, with the goal to derive a Jewish principle and providing a moral lesson. See page 47.

- **Mishnah** — The first written compilation of Jewish oral laws and traditions known as the 'Oral Torah' compiled by Rabbi Yehuda Hanasi before 217 CE. See page 141.

- **Nefesh** — Hebrew word meaning 'Soul'/ 'conscious'/ or 'spirit'. See page 17.

- **Neshama** — Hebrew word for 'Soul'. See page 103.

- **Ohr L'Goyim** — Hebrew phrase meaning a 'light unto other individuals' or a 'shining example to others'. See page 55.

- **Oy l'rasha/ Oy l'shcheino** — Hebrew phrase that translates, 'Woe to the evildoer, woe to his neighbor'. See page 129.

- **Parsha/ Parshas** — Hebrew word meaning 'portion'. It refers to the section of the Torah that is read weekly. See page 109.

- **Pasuk** — Hebrew word for 'verse'. See page 109.

- **Perek** — Hebrew word for 'chapter'. See page 109.

- **Pesachim** — The name for one of the tractates of the Talmud that discusses the holiday of Passover. See page 27.

- **Pirkei Avot** — Translated as 'Chapters of the Fathers'. It is a compilation of the ethical teachings and proverbs of the Rabbis from the Mishnaic period (before 200 CE). See page 37.

- **Rachmonos** — Hebrew word meaning 'having compassion and mercy'. See page 101.

- **Ramban** — The acronym for Rabbi Moses ben Nachman/ Nachmanides, (1194–c. 1270) who was a leading Jewish scholar, rabbi, philosopher, Kabbalist, physician, and commentator. See page 19.

- **Rashi** — The acronym for Rabbi Solomon Yitzchaki (1040 – 1105), who was a scholar, rabbi, and commentator on the Tanach and Talmud. See page 17.

- **Ratzon** — Hebrew word meaning 'willingness'. See page 115.

- **Rav. Od Yosef Chai** — Hebrew statement made by the patriarch Jacob upon learning that his son, Joseph, was still alive, meaning 'I have happiness, Joseph still lives' Genesis (45:26). See page 37.

- **Rebbe** — Hebrew word for 'my mentor/ my teacher'. See page 27.

- **Shabbat/Shabbos** — Hebrew word for the 'Sabbath'. See page 51.

- **Shalom** — Hebrew word for 'peace'/ 'goodbye'/ 'hello'. See page 61.

- **Shechinah** — Hebrew word for 'holiness of God'. See page 53.

- **Shema Yisroel** — Hebrew phrase, "Hear, O Israel: Hashem is our God, Hashem is the One and Only" (Deuteronomy 6:4). See page 63.

- **Shemonei Esreh** — The silent devotion prayer also known as the 'Amidah,' recited standing, three times a day, and four times every Sabbath and Jewish festival. See page 67.

- **Talmid Chacham** — Hebrew word meaning 'student of a wise person.' Used when referring to a scholar and/ or learned person, because every wise person continues to learn from others. See page 127.

- **Talmud** — The Oral Law, which was written down to explain the 'Mishnah' and completed around 500 CE. See page 27.

- **Tanach** — Hebrew acronym for the "Five Books of Moses, the Prophets, and the Writings/ Scrolls", which is commonly referred to as the Old Testament. See page 65.

- **Tanya** — Compilation of works written by the first Lubavitcher Rebbi, Rabbi Schneur Zalman of Liadi Z'TL. See page 13.

- **Teshuvah** — Hebrew word for 'returning' or 'repenting'. See page 135.

- **Torat Chaim** — Hebrew phrase that is translated as the "guidebook to life' or 'the living Torah'. See page 55.

- **Tov I'tzadik, Tov I'shcheino** — Hebrew phrase that translates as, 'Good to the righteous person, good to his neighbor'. See page 131.

- **Tov Meod** — Hebrew phrase literally meaning 'very good'. See page 19.

- **Vayerah** — A parsha/ portion of the Torah, from the book of Bereshit/ Genesis 18:1 through 22:24. See page 109.

- **Veahavta lereacha komocha** — Hebrew phrase that translates as, 'And you should love your neighbor as you love yourself'. See page 37.

- **Vilna Gaon** — Hebrew name meaning 'Genius from Vilnius' describing the sage, scholar, and commentator, Rabbi Elijah ben Solomon Zalman (1720 – 1797). See page 45.

- **V'loh taturu** — Hebrew phrase from Numbers (15:39) that literally means "and do not explore". See page 75.

- **Yetzer Tov/Yetzer Rah** — Hebrew words describing our inclinations/desires for good (tov) or evil (rah). See page 15.

- **Yirat/ Yiras Hashem** — Hebrew phrase meaning 'fear of God' or 'to see and recognize God'. See page 147.

- **Z'TL** — Hebrew acronym abbreviation for the phrase, 'Zecher Tzadik Livracha', which translates as, 'May the memory of this righteous person be a blessing'. See page 27.